Jean Tennant's

"WRITING YOUR LIFE STORY"

Course Materials

Published by: Shapato Publishing
PO Box 476
Everly, IA 51338

ISBN: 978-0-9821058-6-3
Copyright © 2009 Shapato Publishing

All rights reserved. No part of this book may be reproduced or transmitted in any form or by any means, electronic or mechanical, including photocopying, recording, or by an information storage and retrieval system, without permission in writing from the publisher.

First Printing August 2009

SYLLABUS

THE AUTHOR'S LIFESTYLE

QUALITIES NEEDED TO BECOME A SUCCESSFUL WRITER

WRITERS' EQUIPMENT AND SUPPLIES

WHY WRITE YOUR LIFE STORY?
    The Difference between Autobiography and Memoir / The Bubble Method

SHARPENING YOUR WRITING SKILLS
    Word Selection / Sentence Structure / Paragraph Structure / Self-Editing

MANUSCRIPT DEVELOPMENT
    The 3-Act Structure / Story & Plot

BRINGING UP THE PAST / THE PRIVACY OF OTHERS
    Interviewing / Setting / Legal Issues

MANUSCRIPT MECHANICS
    Formatting

SUBMITTING YOUR WORK
    Finding the Right Publisher / Writing a Query Letter or Cover Letter / Multiple Submissions? / Realistic Expectations

LITERARY AGENTS – DO YOU NEED ONE?

THE AUTHOR'S CONTRACT

PROTECTING YOUR WORK
    How to Copyright Your Manuscript

QUESTION AND ANSWER SESSION

PARTICIPANTS' WORK-SHARING SESSION

THE AUTHOR'S LIFESTYLE

2. Solitude

    Are you prepared to spend long periods of time sequestered?

2. Questions

    People will want to know what you're working on. It's up to you to decide if you want to answer those questions.

2. Criticism

    Is your family supportive?

2. Time factor

    It can take months or even years to write a full-length book. Are you prepared for that?

2. Facing Rejection

    It's inevitable, and painful. Can you take it?

> There are three rules for writing. Unfortunately, no one can agree what they are.
>   - Somerset Maugham

QUALITIES NEEDED TO BE A SUCCESSFUL WRITER

IDEAL PERSONAL QUALITIES

1. The Dream / The Desire / Determination
2. Curiosity
3. Organizational Ability
4. Self-Discipline
5. Dedication to Factual Accuracy
6. Persistence / Perseverance
7. Ability to Work Alone
8. Inspiration
9. Enthusiasm
10. Ability to Work Under Pressure
11. Willingness to Accept Constructive Criticism
12. Cooperative Nature
13. Patience
14. Perspective
15. Energy
16. Survival Money

> Anybody can have ideas--the difficulty is to express them without squandering a quire of paper on an idea that ought to be reduced to one glittering paragraph.
> - Mark Twain

TECHNICAL SKILLS

1. Command of English language: spelling, punctuation, etc.
2. Ability to clearly communicate your ideas in writing
3. Knowledge of Manuscript Format
4. Knowledge of the Markets
5. Keyboarding Ability

THE WRITER'S EQUIPMENT AND SUPPLIES

SUGGESTED EQUIPMENT AND SUPPLIES

1. An Idea
2. Paper
3. Envelopes
4. Word Processing Program or Typewriter
5. Ideas File
6. Information File
7. Quiet Place to Write
8. Reference Books

    a. Dictionary / Thesaurus

    b. Style Manual

    c. Specific Books in Your Subject Area

    d. Books that describe how to write your particular type of material

    e. Market Guides

9. Printer or Access to Copy Machine
10. Program or Book to Record Expenses
11. Personalized Business Stationery (optional)
12. Business Cards (optional)

> The Six Golden Rules of Writing:
> Read, read read, and write, write, write.
> - Ernest Gaines

WHY WRITE YOUR LIFE STORY?

Maybe you've been thinking of writing your life story for many years. Or perhaps something happened recently to get you thinking about it. Do people tell you you've had an interesting, unique life? Do you like to share stories about your life and/or your family?

Any of these are legitimate reasons to start writing your own life story.

Short or Long?

Perhaps you're thinking about writing your life story as a full-length book, but if that seems too big a task at this time, consider writing your story in brief increments. Magazines and newspapers are always looking for engaging true accounts of people's lives.

- Essays. The market for essays remains strong. Magazines buy them by the hundreds every year. Accounts of slice-of-life, everyday situations are bought by *Guideposts*, *Redbook*, *Self*, and many other magazines. You might highlight just one period of your life—the early years of your marriage, your college years, fourth grade. The possibilities are endless.

- Nostalgia: Local newspapers and nostalgia-themed magazines are especially interested in hearing from writers who can describe what life was like "way back when."

- Personal Experience: Has something truly amazing happened to you? If so, people will want to hear about it. This could be an adventure you had, a hardship you overcame, a harrowing experience you survived.

> When disaster causes the familiar ground to shudder beneath the feet of a child, a neurotic is sometimes born, or a writer, and often both.
> *Time* magazine, May 20, 1957

Autobiography or Memoir?

An autobiography is the story of your life from birth to the present. A memoir, on the other hand, might cover only a portion of your life. As a writer you could write several memoirs, if you choose.

Some recent bestselling memoirs:

- *The Glass Castle* by Jeannette Walls
  The author chronicles her upbringing at the hands of eccentric, nomadic parents. She and her siblings had to take care of themselves by stealing food at school and living by their wits.

- *A Child Called It* by David Pelzer
  As a young boy Pelzer was starved, stabbed, and smashed face-first into mirrors, yet he rose above the nightmare of his early years to become a responsible adult, family man and successful author.

- *When You Are Engulfed in Flames* by David Sedaris
  Sedaris has written several memoirs, seeming to have the ability to take even the most mundane experiences and make them hilarious.

The Bubble Method

The Bubble Method is simple, and can be used for all types of writing. But it works particularly well with memoir writing. If you're brainstorming for a book, a chapter, an article topic or ideas that you may be interested in writing, the Bubble Method can help. It also works well in developing plots and characters, and even for coming up with a title.

As you get ready to work on your Bubble, ask yourself these questions:

- Who were the strangest characters I met?

- What family or ethnic traditions influenced me as I was growing up?

- How do they still influence me today?

- What turning points changed my life's course?

- What important choices have I made?

- What is my deepest secret?

- What am I most proud of?

- Which persons from my past do I miss most? Dislike most? Value most?

Now, to use the Bubble Method:

1. Take a piece of paper and print "My Life" in the middle of it. If you already know you're interested in focusing on a certain part of your life, such as Junior High, or My First Child, then start with that. Draw a circle around your words, then add ten lines out from the circle, or your first Bubble.

2. Don't censor yourself, don't stop to think. At the end of each outward line, print ten subtopics that are related to your main topic, and draw a circle around them.

3. Brainstorm until you have ten subtopics. If you come up with more than ten don't stop—keep adding them until you run out.

4. Sit back and look at all the fresh ideas or topics the Bubble Method has produced. Absorb what you see there. Memories will churn to the surface.

5. Look at your Bubbles for a few minutes, then select those that seem to support an entire chapter of a book. If you only keep eight or nine, that's okay.

6. Take each of the sub-Bubbles individually and Bubble again. With this second go-round you'll actually be outlining your chapters and will come up with seven to ten main topics for each chapter.

7. Lastly, put the material you've gathered in chronological order. You've now outlined your memoir!

The Characters in Your Life Story

When you worked on your Bubble you undoubtedly thought of several people in your life who have influenced you. You will want to include them in your story.

Fill in a Character Worksheet for each of the people in your story. This includes *yourself!*

Who to Include:
- Important family members
- Influential teachers
- Colorful characters

Who to Leave Out:
- Anyone who doesn't move your story forward.

"I" Can Easily Be Overused

Yes, it is *your* story and should be written in the first person. But you have to be careful that you don't pepper your text too liberally with the "I" word.

An example: "I cried when we left our home in Minnesota and moved to Florida. I loved our little town in Minnesota. I liked hanging out at the theater with my friends. I never tired of driving the loop with them. I even liked going to visit my grandparents' at their house across town."

Rewrite this paragraph, a sentence at a time or combining them if you wish:

- I cried when we left our home in Minnesota and moved to Florida.

- I loved our little town in Minnesota.

- I liked hanging out at the theater with my friends.

- I never tired of driving the loop with them.

- I even liked going to visit my grandparents at their house across town.

SHARPENING YOUR WRITING SKILLS

Word Selection

Use words that convey what you want them to say.

Use words that have precise meaning.

Use short, simple, easy-to-understand words instead of long, complicated, or technical words.

Don't write down to your readers.

Select words that are within your readers' comprehension level.

Visualize a scene or event, then select words to accurately describe it. Paint word-pictures . . . but don't forget the other senses.

Avoid unnecessary words.

Attributive clauses. When writing dialogue, balance descriptive words and phrases with "said."

"I got a new job," my Aunt Irma _____.

"I don't think that's fair," Billy _____.

"I'm going to become a doctor," my brother Danny _____.

"I've gained twenty-five pounds in the last two months," Mom _____.

"Where are you going?" my mother _____.

"I suppose you're right," Grandfather _____.

> Better to write for yourself and have no public, than to write for the public and have no self.
> - Cyril Connolly

Dialogue should always accomplish at least one of these five functions—move the story along, reveal the past, develop or reveal character, clarify theme, or define tone. If it doesn't do at least one of these things it's probably unnecessary and should be cut.

Writing Dialect

Writing in an accent or dialect can be tricky, even for seasoned professionals. If you try to mirror how people in your early life actually talked, it can make the reading of it impossible.

Sentence Structure

- If you don't know rules of grammar, sentence structure and punctuation, look for examples.

- Use simple, rather than complicated, sentence structure.

- Use sentence structure you can handle.

- Vary sentence length.

> From "The Natural," by Josh Hamilton, *Guideposts* magazine, 6/09/2009
>
> The light changed. I couldn't keep my news bottled up any longer. "The manager told me if it were up to him, I'd be breaking camp with the big-league team," I blurted out. I paused a second before adding that the team's executives had overruled the manager. For now.

- Write as you would talk, but without the excess words.

- Use active, rather than passive, sentences.
    Passive: The 50-yard touchdown pass was thrown by Chuck.
    Active: Chuck threw the 50-yard touchdown pass.

Defining Passive Voice

Passive voice occurs when the subject and object of an action are inverted, so the subject is the recipient of the act instead of its performer. For example:

Passive: The man was bitten by the dog.
Active: The dog bit the man.

Passive: I was told by the interviewer to come at noon.
Active: The interviewer told me to come at noon.

Note that the word "by" is present in these two examples. A sentence can be passive without the word "by," but it is always at least implied. For example: "I was given bad directions [by my friend]."

When Passive Voice is Acceptable

There are generally two cases when passive voice is acceptable: 1) when there is no defined or tangible subject; 2) when the emphasis really should be on the object of the action. In these cases, the alternative is often awkward and sounds less natural.

Case 1: He is called 'the great one.'
Awkward alternative: "The general public calls him 'the great one.'"

Case 2: "For the fifth time this year, Jefferson was hit by a pitch."
Awkward alternative: "For the fifth time this year, a pitch hit Jefferson."

- Avoid clichés and jargon.

- Don't overwork the same words (redundancies).

- Write for clarity, meaning, and understanding instead of eloquent, but hollow, beauty.

- Respect your own "voice."

> Don't tell me the moon is shining. Show me the glint of light on broken glass.
> - Anton Chekhov

> **Choose Strong Action Verbs**
>
> Active language comes not just from avoiding passive voice but further requires the use of *strong action verbs*. In addition to avoiding *to be* verbs, you should try to replace helping verbs such as *have, had, has, do, does, did* and other vague verbs like *got* and *get*.
>
> **Before:** "I **had** opportunities to develop my skills."
> **After:** "I **sought** opportunities to develop my skills."
>
> **Before:** "I **got** the promotion through hard work."
> **After:** "I **earned** the promotion through hard work."
>
> **Before:** "She **did well** in this competitive environment."
> **After:** "She **thrived** in this competitive environment."
>
> **Before:** "My mother **didn't want** to show up without a gift."
> **After:** "My mother **hesitated** to show up without a gift."
>
> **Before:** "The salesman **told** the audience about his products."
> **After:** "The salesman **promoted** his products to the audience."
>
> The last two examples demonstrate the lack of clear distinction between strong and weak verbs. *Promoted* is simply a stronger word than *told*, and brings the writing to life.

Paragraph Structure

- Present one main topic per paragraph.

- Use short paragraphs.

- Each sentence in a paragraph should flow smoothly into the next.

- Each paragraph should flow smoothly into the next.

Self-Editing Your Work

- After you finish your manuscript, set it aside for a time.

- Read your work aloud.

- Scrutinize each word, sentence and paragraph.

- Read for content and meaning.

- Check spelling, punctuation and mechanics.

- Check for redundancies.

- Ask yourself these questions:

    Is the sequence of the events and topics logical?
    Is the theme believable?
    Will a reader get a crystal-clear meaning of my idea?
    Is the format consistent?
    Is the tone consistent?

- Don't stop revising until your work is the best you can make it.

- Expect to revise and rewrite your work 3, 4, 5 times or *more*.

- Don't over-edit; seeking perfection can suck the life out of your words.

Hone Your Writing Skills

- Take college courses.

- Attend seminars and workshops.

- Read books and magazine articles about writing.

- Read and study the type of work you intend to write.

- Take online courses in writing, such as those offered by:

    Writer's Digest
    www.writersonlineworkshops.com

- Join online writers' groups, such as:

    Coffeehouse for Writers
    www.coffeehouseforwriters.com

    Critique Circle
    www.critiquecircle.com

    The National Writer's Association
    www.NationalWriters.com

- Start your own writers' group.

- If you want to be a writer, write!

    Personal letters to friends and relatives

    Keep a journal

    Volunteer to help prepare a newsletter, brochure, or other publication for charitable organizations or a church

    Write your family history

    Write letters to the editor

> Close the door. Write with no one looking over your shoulder. Don't try to figure out what other people want to hear from you; figure out what you have to say.
> - Barbara Kingsolver

MANUSCRIPT DEVELOPMENT

GENERAL GUIDELINES

Format

Format is the arrangement of the parts of the manuscript.

- For nonfiction, devise a system of units, chapters and other appropriate dividers.

- Devise a system of headings and subheadings.

- Develop an order for your manuscript. Present like materials in the same way under the same heading levels.

- Be consistent with your format throughout the manuscript.

- Consider how you will use examples, sidebars, illustrations and the like.

Content

Content is what is included in your manuscript. Decide how thoroughly you will explain each topic.

- The makeup of your reader audience and the nature of your topic will provide a good guide.

- Be as concise as possible. Do not tell everything you know. Provide only that which is absolutely necessary for the reader to be told.

- Do not leave out essential information that must be revealed to the reader in order for them to reach the proper conclusion.

Style

Style is your voice, how you express your ideas.

- Develop your own personal style/voice.

- Use a writing style that is within generally acceptable limits.
- Write in a style that is normal for the type of work you are preparing.
- If you are preparing a manuscript for submission to a particular publication, gear your writing toward the writing style found in that publication.

Outlining

You used the Bubble Method to outline your story. There are still some basic rules you'll want to be aware of. The Three-Act Structure is a rule that most novels are written following. Being aware of the Three-Act Structure can help you put together a compelling memoir as well.

Act 1

1. Hook: A gripping plot event that draws the reader into the story.
2. Backstory: A bridge that introduces the protagonist and lays the groundwork for plot and story.
3. Trigger: An event that propels the protagonist into crisis.

Act 2

1. Crisis: The protagonist suffers an emotional crisis because of the trigger's effect on a character flaw.
2. Struggle: The protagonist struggles against ever-increasing obstacles.
3. Epiphany: The protagonist realizes his/her flaw and overcomes it (or not).

Act 3

1. Plan: The protagonist does something he/she couldn't do before the epiphany.
2. Climax: The protagonist confronts the antagonist, who (or which) is defeated.
3. Ending: The plot and story conflicts are resolved, and the reader is left satisfied.

> It's impossible to discourage the real writers. They don't give a damn what you say, they're going to write.
> - Sinclair Lewis

STORY & PLOT

Without a story, your novel is nothing more than a series of events. And without those events the emotions of the characters—and mainly you—would exist in a meaningless context. A memoir, as does a novel, needs both events (plot) and story to keep your readers captivated.

STORY is emotional. When you feel sad, that's part of the story. Some elements of story are:

Anger * Joy * Fear * Desire * Sorrow

PLOT is physical. When you yell, strike out, laugh, that's part of the plot. Some elements of plot are:

Plan * Speed * Danger * Thrills * Conflict

It's important to balance plot and story. You need both and one leads naturally to the other. Here's a rough example of how a memoir would include both:

Plot:
After accidentally setting a fire and burning up my father's prized car, (Hook)

Story:
I was afraid he would never speak to me again.

All the previous summer, when I'd turned twelve, we'd worked on that car together, and doing so had brought us closer. (Backstory)

Plot:
My family blamed the fire on some hobos who'd come through town recently, which

Story:
added to my feelings of guilt. I envied the hobos their life, free of burdens and responsibility.

Plot:
I decided to run away from home, (Trigger)

Story:
too ashamed to face my family with my terrible secret.

Plot:
That night I packed my most prized possessions in a small duffle bag and climbed out the bedroom window,

Story:
afraid now that if caught, this would make matters worse. (Crisis)

Plot:
I reached the edge of town and hopped on a slow-moving train. There I encountered several of the hobos, also on their way out of town. They'd heard they were being accused of setting a fire, and have decided it's time to leave.

Story:
I believe I'll fit right in with them, as I now consider myself an outsider as well.

Plot:
When they hop off the train a couple of days later, I get off with them,

Story:
excited about this new turn of events and the direction my life is going.

Plot:
But the hobo camp is a miserable, dangerous place.

Story:
I miss my family, and had underestimated their capacity for understanding. (Epiphany)

Plot:
I tell the hobos I'm going to return home, but they won't let me leave.

Story:
Feeling stronger through self-discovery, I wait until they are all asleep, (Plan)

Plot:
then sneak away from the camp. One hobo wakes and sounds the alarm, but I am able to grab my few belongings and escape from the camp. (Climax)

Story:
With newfound confidence (Ending)

Plot:
I return home and to my relieved family

Story:
happy to be back with the people I love and ready to confess my part in the fire.

END

Titles

Follow these guidelines in selecting a title for your manuscript.

1. Whether short or long, make it catchy and attention-getting.

2. Use a subtitle, in nonfiction, to more fully explain the title and the manuscript.

3. Make the title relevant. The title should reflect the content of the article or book.

4. Don't be so clever that the average reader cannot understand the title or can't draw the association between title and manuscript content.

Production Rate

Production rate refers to the volume of material produced in a given time.

1. There is no standard production rate. Some successful authors regularly spend days on a single paragraph. Others routinely crank out a romance novel every couple of months.

2. To produce an adequate volume of material, follow these suggestions:
   a. Write regularly. Set aside a time to write each day or each week, and stick to your schedule.
   b. Set a goal of a certain number of pages per day or per week.

Use of a Pseudonym

A pseudonym is a pen name under which an author's works are published.

Why Use a Pseudonym?
1. To protect a writer's identity from friends, business associates, etc.

2. If your real name is 'plain'

3. For different types of works

Selecting a Pen Name

1. Do not select a pen name used by another published author.
    a. Check the Library of Congress Catalog Directory of Authors at a library.
    b. Enter a name in Amazon.com and see what comes up.

2. Do not select the name of a famous person.

3. If you select a real person's name, change the spelling or use a selection or combination of names.

BRINGING UP THE PAST

INTERVIEWING RELATIVES AND OTHER IMPORTANT PLAYERS

You can't write your life story without the assistance of other. As you prepare to interview family members you might run into resistance. Not everyone will want to be a part of a documented account of the past. You might run into obstacles because of:

1. Scandal. Is there something scandalous in your family history that others will want kept hidden?

2. Embarrassment. Most people have incidents in their past they'd rather keep in the past.

THE INVERVIEW

Make an appointment. Don't spring it on people.

1. Prepare a list of questions. This will help you stay focused on the responses rather than wondering what you're going to ask next. Keep your questions in chronological order – don't jump around.

2. Tape-record the interview. You can't write fast enough to get it all down, and by tape recording you'll have an accurate record of exactly what your subject said.

3. Ask questions that involve the senses:
   a. The smell of your mother's perfume
   b. The smell of the family kitchen before supper
   c. The sound of your grandfather's voice
   d. The pattern on your grandmother's dress

4. Ask questions designed to elicit a detailed answer:
   a. How did you feel when…?
   b. What happened when…?

5. Near the end of your interview ask: "Is there anything you'd like to add or talk about that we haven't covered?" Don't assume your subject will bring up important details on their own.

CHARACTERS

We talked about the characters in your story in an earlier section. While they are important, don't forget that this is *your* story, and however colorful the characters in your life were, the focus should remain on you.

RESEARCH

This is a big part of writing your memoir. Besides interviews and photographs, there are site that can help you remember what was happening in your life during a certain period in time. You may want to know what movies you went to, which television shows you watched, what songs on the radio were popular at the time.

Sites for researching years past:

> www.dmarie.com/timecap
>
> www.thepeoplehistory.com
>
> www.ancestry.com

PHOTOGRAPHS

Old photographs are a great way to bring back memories, and also to get a description of how things looked in the past. Examine photographs to fill in the details of your story:

- Clothes. What were the styles? Hats. Dresses. Men's suits. Shoes.
- Hairstyles. How did your mother wear her hair? Your grandmother? You?

YOUR SENSORY MEMORY

As you're researching your past for your memoir, don't forget to include all of the senses. Dig deep to bring the past to life:

- What did your kitchen smell like?
- What was the view from your bedroom window?
- What did your grandparents' voices sound like?
- The feel of your pet's fur against your cheek?

LOCATION:

Describe the locations in which your life story occurs. This will help your readers know you, and help them share your experiences. Details make the story.

> Instead of writing:
>
> Our house was located on Main Street. It was small and square, with a fence around the yard. I didn't like the way it looked.
>
> Write:
>
> Even though Mom had spent most of last summer painting our small, square house a cheerful yellow, the paint was already faded and peeling. Two of the white shutters hung crooked, a result of a recent thunderstorm. The fence that surrounded the yard was rusted. Sometimes, coming home from school, I walked right past it and tried to pretend, for a few minutes, that I didn't live there.

More resources to help you research:

    www.infoplease.com
    www.livinghistoryfarm.org

> The future belongs to those who believe in the beauty of their dreams.
> - Eleanor Roosevelt

THE PRIVACY OF OTHERS

You'll have to make your own decisions about the writer's (your) responsibility to those whose lives are entwined with your own. You might want to write about a failed romance, or the end of your marriage. Perhaps your memoir will involve your closeted gay aunt, your teenage son's brief drug use, or a close friend's arrest for embezzlement. You must balance your reasons for writing this story against the harm you might be doing to another person.

If you publish a story that includes details of a neighbor who is an illegal immigrant, a teacher who was having an affair with a student, a family doctor who assisted in a suicide, you may become responsible for someone's deportation or job loss, financial ruin or social ostracism, if the characters are recognizable. As writers it's our business to fully understand what can happen to people when we reveal what we know about them.

Writing about those who have hurt us is a different matter. We may find ourselves not caring, or even delighting in, the consequences to family members, priests, medical professionals, teachers, and others who have abused their power over us in the past.

But beware of revenge as a motive:

- Writing that has retaliation as its goal is always transparent, and makes readers uncomfortable.

- Although anger may be what gets you started, your writing will not flourish until you give your full allegiance to the story itself, and let go of your wish to gain sympathy from readers or to hurt someone.

Finally, be honest! If you're going to strip bare the lives of other people, then it wouldn't be fair to be less honest about your own flaws and wrongdoings.

YOUR MEMOIR AND THE LAW

Many writers engaged in writing memoir worry about being sued. But it is a genuine legal concern for only a few. The chances of your being sued are small. It practically never happens. Aside from the question of whether there are legal grounds for a lawsuit, there are two very good reasons why you are unlikely to face a legal challenge.

1. It's very expensive to bring a lawsuit. It's so expensive in fact, that it's beyond the means of most people—though hiring a lawyer to *threaten* a not beyond the means of many. Even when a lawyer is to be paid not on an hourly basis but with a percentage of the amount won the in the suit, the person suing will have to pay a lot of expenses such as filing feels, expert witness, depositions and so on. Most lawyers won't even take such a case unless they feel very confident about winning large reward.

2. Secondly, most people who may dislike your version of events or your portrayal of them do not want to bring even more attention to what you have said, although the lawsuit gives them the opportunity to refute it.

Don't worry about your legal situation while you're writing your memoir. The time to consider it is when you are ready to publish. And that brings us to:

- Most publishing company contracts require to you indemnify your publisher against any claims of defamation or invasions of privacy, which means that if they are sued, you will have to pay. However, no publisher wants to rely on collecting from an author in such a situation like that, and they will first consult their own legal counsel to make sure there are no potential problems.

There are two general areas of the law that apply to your writings:

Defamation

Defamation laws, which include libel (written defamation) and slander (spoken defamation) are concerned with the publication of *false* information about a person that causes damage to his or her reputation and/or ability to succeed in a business. Examples might include statements regarding criminal conduct, gross immorality, bankruptcy or insolvency, Ku Klux Klan membership, etc. These are civil laws—not criminal—under which the person claiming to be harmed by your writing must bring a civil lawsuit against you.

To be legally ruled defamatory, a statement in your memoir must be:

- *False*. A statement that can be proved true is not defamatory. If you write that your father used to beat you as a child, and he claims this is a lie, you would only need a relative or two willing to back up your claim.

- *Published.* The statement must be communicated publicly.

- *Stated as fact.* Statements that clearly represent an opinion rather than a fact are relatively safe from defamation suits. If you write "I thought my father was the meanest man in three counties," that's an opinion.

- *About a named or identifiable person.* Your statement is considered defamatory only when the person is named or recognizable because of his/her personality, physical description, or other identifying characteristics. Defamation can also be claimed by groups when your statement can be shown to inure a whole group or one of its members.

- *About a living person.* Generally speaking, no one can sue on behalf of a dead person.

- *Damaging or injurious to the person concerned.* For it to be defamatory, your statement must cause the person to be held in public contempt or hatred, or must interfere with his/her ability to succeed financially or professionally, or must cause him/her to lose a spouse.

Invasion of Privacy / Protection of Personality Rights

"Invasion of Privacy" is an umbrella concept that can encompass several quite different situations that would apply to the author. It involves:

- *The publication of offensive or embarrassing private facts* about an identifiable person—facts that are not already a matter of public record. The definition of what is offensive or embarrassing is based on the 'community standards' of your locale.

- *Using facts in a way that conveys a person in a false light.* This is different from defamation in that here the facts are used to mislead, though the facts may be true.

- *Using someone's name or picture for commercial gain* without consent. For example, if someone about whom you write in your memoir is famous or has a proprietary, money-making interest in her or his name, image, photographic likeness, etc., you should be cautious about using any of those in your memoir if you plan to publish it for profit. In such cases, it's a good idea to get written permission.

Again, bearing in mind that the likelihood of anyone suing you is low, there are precautions you can take:

1. *Tell the truth.* Since it may be difficult to prove in some instances, wherever possible research your facts and keep accurate records of your research. Especially when making accusations against people, make sure you have hard evidence to back your claims.

2. *Express your opinions as opinions.* Be careful not to state opinions as facts.

3. *Attribute controversial statements to others.* If sources other than you can verify your version of a story that might provoke someone, it's good to quote your sources, particularly if they're known to be reliable. However, you are still ultimately responsible for what you say and phrases such as 'it is alleged' are unlikely to protect you if you make questionable statements.

4. *Get consent from those you write about.* Getting a written release if you can is always a good idea. Consult a writer's legal resource for examples. There are several, all found on Amazon.com. A good resource is:
    a. *The Writer's Legal Companion* by Brad Bunnin and Peter Beren.

5. *Change names and disguise people.* If you're concerned about the consequences, legal or otherwise, of publishing a story that might upset people, try making them unrecognizable.

6. *Don't worry forever.* There's a statute of limitations that varies from state to state. In most cases it's one or two years from the date of publication, after which you cannot be sued.

Now that we've covered some of these touchy areas, go ahead and write your memoir and don't stress about these issues until you are ready to be published. Don't worry about it while you are writing, and don't confuse your nervousness about telling your story with worry about the unlikely possibility of legal consequences.

Writing and publishing are two separate stages of your work. Deal with them one at a time.

MANUSCRIPT MECHANICS

MANUSCRIPTS FOR BOOKS AND MAGAZINES

Use this format for preparing manuscripts for books, magazine articles, shorts stories and novels.

Paper

1. White, 8 ½" x 11", 20 pound weight.

2. No erasable bond.

Word Processor or Typewriter

1. Use a good, letter-quality inkjet or laser printer. Do not use a dot matrix printer.

2. If using a typewriter, use a good, fresh ribbon.

3. If using a typewriter, pica is preferred over elite.

4. If using a typewriter, erasing, strike-over paper or liquid paper is acceptable. If there are several error corrections per page, retype. If using a computer and printer, reprint.

5. Use a standard type style. Times New Roman is preferred; Arial is acceptable. Do not use script, italics or unusual styles. The exception is italics for the emphasis of individual words.

Format

1. Type on one side of the paper only.

2. Double-space the entire manuscript.

3. A title page can be used for a book manuscript. Include the manuscript title, your name and address, the approximate word count.

4. On page two and subsequent pages, leave about one inch as a top margin above the page number. After the page number, triple space before resuming the manuscript.

5. Set side margins at 1 ¼ to 1 ½" wide.

6. Set bottom margin at 1 ¼ to 1 ½" inches.

> Writers are always selling somebody out.
> - Joan Didion

(Sample Title Page)

Mary Jones Memoir
125 Orchard Lane 60,000 words
Midwest, IA 51xxx
712-xxx-xxxx
MJJones@sample.com

MY YEAR AS A NANNY:

Child Care for the Rich and Famous in Hollywood

By Mary Jones

Mary Jones
125 Orchard Lane
Midwest, IA 51xxx
712-xxx-xxxx
MJJones@sample.com

Approx. 4,200 words

MY YEAR AS A NANNY:
Child Care for the Rich and Famous in Hollywood

By Mary Jones

Use this format for the first page of your magazine article, short story, newspaper article or children's picture book. The title is placed one-third of the way down the page. If a pseudonym is used, it appears in the byline and the writer's real name is shown in the return address area in the upper left-hand corner. Show the approximate number of words

---

MY YEAR AS A NANNY / Jones   2

Several different styles are acceptable for the second page heading of your manuscript. Here's one. Whatever format you use, make sure you use it consistently on every page of your manuscript.

Leave a one-inch top margin above the heading on page two and subsequent pages. After the heading, triple space, leaving two blank lines before continuing with the text of the manuscript.

SUBMITTING YOUR WORK

QUERY LETTERS

A query letter is sent to a publisher or literary agent. It serves to briefly describe your manuscript idea and asks if you may submit more material for an editor's review. Note: some publishers / agents prefer that you submit the first three chapters of your work, or even the entire work with your letter. Check market guides for editorial preferences.

Finding the Right Publisher

1. Know your manuscript.
    a. What is its topic and slant?
    b. To what type of reader will it appeal?
    c. For what publishing medium is it best suited?

2. Familiarize yourself with publishers that publish your type of work.
    a. Browse through bookstores and libraries.
    b. Browse Amazon.com and BarnesandNoble.com.
    c. Check the *Subject Guide to Books in Print*.
    d. Check your local library.
    e. Check market guidebooks like *Writer's Market* and *Literary Marketplace*.

3. From a market guide, determine publisher's attitudes toward queries and their requirements for submitting them. Adhere to their requests.

4. Make a list of potential publishers, complete with addresses and editors' names. Rank them in category, from most ideal to least ideal.

5. Query the most ideal publishers first.

6. Consider making multiple queries.

Query Letter Philosophies and Procedures

The information below provides perspectives and philosophies about query letters and describes how to use them.

Purpose of the Query Letter

1. Present your idea and sell the editor on its being a good idea.
2. Demonstrate your writing ability.
3. Obtain permission to submit more material.
4. Begin a dialogue with an editor.

Manuscript Development Before Query

1. With a non-fiction book, you can send a query letter and proposal after developing your basic idea and slant.
2. With fiction, for a beginning writer, you are expected to complete the entire manuscript before querying.
3. With a short story, you should have the manuscript completed.
4. With a short magazine article, you should have the manuscript completed.
5. With a long magazine article, you should, at a minimum, have your theme and slant developed.

Content of Query Letter

1. If you have impressive publishing credits, emphasize them.
2. Summarize the manuscript topic.
3. Explain your particular approach.
4. Evaluate the project's relevance.

5. Estimate the project's completed length.

6. Include whether or not the project is completed.

7. Summarize your background.

8. You may include one or more of the following:
   a. Synopsis / Outline
   b. Market Analysis
   c. Samples of previous publications

Structure of the Query Letter

1. Use white, 8 ½" x 11" bond paper, 20 pound weight. 24 pound acceptable. If you have personalized letterhead paper, you may use it.

2. Limit your letter to one page.

3. Address the letter to a specific editor by name, if possible.

4. Each letter should be original.

5. Demonstrate your writing style and skill.

6. Make certain there are no errors or obvious typographical corrections.

7. Close with a request of some type of action from the editor.

8. Enclose SASE.

9. Be appreciative.

Realistic Expectations

1. You will likely hear from most of the publishers queried. However, you might never hear from some of them.

2. Most responses will be form letters.

3. If your proposal is rejected, it's likely you will not be given a specific reason.

4. If you have selected a good topic and have developed an enticing query letter and proposal, one or more publishers may ask to see your work.

5. If you submit your completed manuscript (or sample), upon an editor's request, you are making progress, but you are still a long way from having a contract.

6. Hang in there!

Follow-Up

1. Normal response time:
   a. Magazines: 6 to 12 weeks.
   b. Books: 3 to 9 months.

2. Follow-up procedure:
   a. Send a follow-up letter after a reasonable time.

Record

1. Maintain records of names and addresses of publishers and the date on which the query letter was sent.

2. Record the publisher response.

3. Record follow-up information.

> If you write one story, it may be bad; if you write a hundred, you have the odds in your favor.
> - Edgar Rice Burroughs

(SAMPLE QUERY LETTER)

Date

Editor's Name, Editorial Assistant (or title)
Name of Company
Street
City, State, Zip

Dear xxxxx:

When I was eighteen years old I accidentally ran over the handsome photographer I'd recently met, breaking his leg. I then spent the rest of my summer vacation driving him around to various photo shoots. A year later we were married, thus beginning the adventure of our life together, traveling the world as my husband pursued his dreams of photographic glory. Though extremely talented and charismatic, he was also, unfortunately, an abusive alcoholic, and it took me nearly fifteen years to find the courage to break free of the hold he had on me. I fled in the middle of the night with our three children, traveling without passports and very little money through some of the most dangerous parts of the Middle East.

AS EAGLES SOAR is my recently completed 60,000-word memoir. Though stories of alcoholism, abuse and hard-earned freedom are all too commonplace, I believe the global setting of my experience makes it stand out from the others.

Enclosed please find a short synopsis and first three chapters of AS EAGLES SOAR. SASE is included for your reply. Thank you for your time, and I look forward to hearing from you.

Sincerely,

Your Name
Address
City, State
Phone
Email

AGENTS

At some point in your writing career, you will probably consider the use of an agent to place your work.

Agent's Activities

1. An agent's job is to place the author's manuscript with the most suitable publisher. Sometimes agents also help promote and publicize the author's work.

2. Agents will handle both established authors with publishing credits to their name, and unpublished writers.

3. Agents usually handle only books, and television and movie scripts. There is not enough money involved in magazine articles, short stories, poetry and the like to make it worth their while.

4. Agents charge 10% to 15% of the author's gross earnings for placing works with a domestic publisher and, usually, another 5% for placing works with a foreign publisher.

5. Some agents charge a reading fee for reviewing a prospective client's manuscript. Respectable agents do not charge reading fees.

How to Find an Agent

1. The following publications contain lists of book and screenplay agents:

    Writer's Market, published by Writer's Digest Books

    Literary Marketplace, published by Information Today

    Guide to Literary Agents published by Writer's Digest Books
    Jeff Herman's Guide to Book Publishers, Editors & Literary Agents by Jeff Herman

Why to Use an Agent

1. Publishers are more willing to look at work submitted by an agent, because they know the work has merit.

2. Your agent will make sure you receive your full royalties due in a timely manner.

3. Your agent will help resolve any creative differences that might arise between you and the publisher.

Why Not to Use an Agent

1. It may be just as difficult and time-consuming to land an agent who will handle your work as it would be to place the work yourself.

2. If you place your work without the aid of an agent, you'll save 10 – 15% of the royalties paid.

3. Even if you land an agent, they may not give you and your work a satisfactory amount of attention.

4. You can gain valuable experience and insight by handling your own marketing.

THE AUTHOR'S CONTRACT

Someday you may be fortunate enough to – finally! – sign a publishing contract. When that day comes, there are a few things you should know.

What the Publisher Agrees to do for You

1. Publish your book within a fixed time frame, usually 12 to 18 months from the time you deliver the signed contract.

2. Allow you to review and correct galley proofs of your work.

3. Consult with you regarding book jacket, blurbs and your author biography and photo.

4. Pay your advances in a prompt manner, and royalties twice a year.

What the Publisher Does NOT Agree to Do

1. Market your book.

2. Give you final say over the book jacket design.

3. Guarantee a certain print run.

What You Agree to Do

1. Deliver a book of an agreed length, genre and subject matter, before the agreed-upon date.

2. Confirm that the book is your original work, and that you aren't libeling anyone with it.

> We are what we repeatedly do. Excellence, therefore, is not an act but a habit.   Aristotle

PROTECTING YOUR WORK

Securing a Copyright

Idea and concepts cannot be copyrighted, but your expression of those ideas can be. That is, the specific combination of words you use to express your ideas and concepts are protected by copyright. Illustrations, photographs and other artwork are also protected by copyright.

Material published after March 1, 1989 is automatically copyrighted when written and doesn't need a copyright notation.

> Even though a copyright notation is not needed, many writers affix the notation anyway, as shown below, when showing their work to the general public, to fend off those who might be tempted to copy their work.
>
> Copyright © 2008, Jean Tennant
>
> Do NOT include the copyright notation when submitting your work to a literary agent or publisher. It's considered the sign of an amateur.

To establish your proof of ownership, register your copyright online at:

> www.copyright.gov

or through the following address:

> U.S. Copyright Office
> Library of Congress
> 101 Independence Avenue, SE
> Washington, DC 20559-6000

Copyright forms are free, available online through the above sources, or you can call 202-707-9100 to request a form. To speak to someone at the copyright office about specific copyright questions,

call 202-707-3000. The correct forms to use to register various types of works are:

> Form TX: Written works, including book manuscripts, magazine articles, short stories and poetry.
>
> Form PA: Plays and music
>
> Form VA: Illustrations and photographs

Send one copy of your work, the completed copyright registration form and a $45 fee to the U.S. Copyright Office. The copyright office will date your copyright applications soon after it is received. You'll receive a copy of the copyright registration, bearing your registration number. It may take as long as six months to receive your copy of the form.

The Berne Convention, ratified by the U.S. Congress in 1989, gives copyright protection in the U.S. and eighty other countries.

A copyright lasts for the author's lifetime plus 70 years. If you have a co-author or collaboration with an illustrator, the copyright lasts the lifetime of the last survivor plus 70 years. If you use a pseudonym, the copyright protection lasts for 100 years or for 75 years after publication, whichever is shorter.

Selling Rights

Various types of serial rights can be sold to works published in magazines and newspapers. The term *serial* means those publications that are published on a continual basis, like magazines and newspapers. Some of the more common serial rights are listed below:

> The term First Serial Rights means that the first rights to publish in the U.S. only are being granted.
>
> The term First North American Serial Rights means that first rights are granted for publication in North America (U.S. and Canada).

The terms <u>Second Serial Rights</u> and <u>Second North American Serial Rights</u> refer to the right to publish a book excerpt in a magazine

after the book is published. The terms also are used to identify subsequent sales to magazines or newspapers of a published article or story where first rights were granted to the original publisher. Second rights can be sold any number of times by the copyright holder.

The term <u>All Rights</u> refers to the sale of all rights to the author's work. Thereafter, the author is unable to sell second rights to other users.

The term <u>One-Time Rights</u> refers to the author's giving a publication permission to publish the material one time, and then all rights revert to the copyright holder. The publisher receives no guarantee that they are the only one, or the first one, to receive permission to publish the material.

The term <u>Simultaneous Rights</u> refers to granting the right to more than one publisher to publish your work, all at the same time or with no regard for who publishes the work first.

#1 MOST IMPORTANT THING TO REMEMBER: NEVER GIVE UP!

> I would credit my success as an author not to any great talent, in particular, but through sheer stubborn determination.

NOTES

NOTES

Made in the USA